emoji puzzles

THIS IS A CARLTON BOOK

Published by Carlton Books Ltd
20 Mortimer Street
London W1T 3JW

Copyright © 2016 Carlton Books Ltd
Emoji artwork supplied by Emoji One (http://emojione.com)

A CIP catalogue for this book is available from the British Library.

Project editor: Charlotte Selby
Design: James Pople and Tokiko Morishima
Production: Sarah Kramer

ISBN 978-1-78739-039-3

Printed in Dubai

10 9 8 7 6 5 4 3 2 1

emoji puzzles

350 ENIGMAS FOR YOU TO SOLVE!

**CARLTON
BOOKS**

Contents

Chapter 3: Sports & Culture

Chapter 4: Trivia & Answers

Welcome to *Emoji Puzzles!*

A couple of years ago, finishing a text or a post with an emoji was considered uncool, childish even. Today, that's changed. Everyone's using them. Even mom. Even grandma! Why? Because emojis are awesome! And they have changed the world for the better ... one round little face at a time.

These little colorful characters have—like it or not—become part of the very fabric of our modern society. We have embraced them in our workplaces, schools and homes. Ninety-two percent of people online now use emoijs every day. How's that for complete and total emoji-mania?!

Now, yes, emojis may sometimes confuse us, annoy us, and often create misunderstandings with our friends and partners, and they may be intrinsically meaningless to us in times of real emotional tragedy, but emojis have become integral to the way we communicate, live and behave these days. They have, rather cleverly, re-introduced emotion back into our digital communication. We are no longer just robots sending "xx" at the end of our text messages—now we can express a whole range of emotions.

From the Broken Heart to the Face Throwing a Kiss, emojis can perfectly sum up how we feel at the touch of a button. We use them as accessories to enhance our style, and they reflect our moods and personality. These colorful, friendly, and useful communication companions continue to fascinate us with each new year, and with every new emoji that is released, they will only become more important to us in the future—a time when, perhaps, we'll only communicate via emojis. Imagine that?

With *Emoji Puzzles* you can now use your emoji-nation to emoji-fy your puzzling power through creative emoji-neering. Basically, that means you can have lots of fun using emojis to solve puzzles from all areas of popular culture. From movies to sport, books to TV, music to history, and art to science; see the world as you've never seen it before... emoji-fied!

While most puzzle books put you to sleep, *Emoji Puzzles*—the first emoji-based book of its kind—will put a smile on your face no matter where you are. So, what are you waiting for? Turn the page and get cracking with the newest and coolest emoji puzzles ever devised.

Use Your Emoji-nation

HOW THE PUZZLES WORK

If you've never done an emoji puzzle before then it's best to start off nice and easy. Just kidding, we're getting straight into it! But they're pretty straightforward, once you know how to work them out. And after that point, emoji puzzles are just simply addictive!

Some are quite easy while others are trickier and may have you scratching your head. We have varied the difficulty levels to make them as fun as possible and have covered a range of topics to really give your brain an emoji workout.

Once you've worked them out and got them right, send them on to a friend using your phone to see if they can solve the puzzles. Or better yet, give them the book when you're done with it.

But before we begin, let's test your emoji-nation and give you a few sample emoji puzzles, just to ease you in. For this section, we'll stick to movies to help you get comfortable. After this, you're on your own!

BEGINNER

ANSWER: *Scary Movie*

Easy, right?

ANSWER: *Snakes on a Plane*

EASY

Fingers or hands pointing forwards or backwards represent words such as "on" or "in." Words such as "the" are always left out, so don't panic if you can't see them.

ANSWER: *Eat Pray Love*

MEDIUM

Some emojis are often deliberately placed to confuse you. The hotdog in this emoji is not actually referring to a hotdog, but to eating in general.

ANSWER: *Midnight in Paris*

HARD

Time and clocks play an important role in emoji puzzles both as timekeepers and for representing numbers. The puzzles will also be testing your general knowledge and may relate to movies that were made decades ago.

ANSWER: *The Curious Case of Benjamin Button*

FOR EMOJI-NATORS ONLY!

And finally ... there are some super advanced puzzles that will push your emoji-nation to the limit. These can be a mix of a literal translation as well as clues relating to the movies' plot or key characters.

Music

Like fish and chips, salt and pepper, and cheese and wine, emojis and music are the perfect combination, the best of friends. In this chapter we have emojified the lyrics of many great songs—transforming once powerful rhyming couplets and deep, soul-searching melancholy into amazing works of emoji art. These emoji music puzzles will get your feet tapping and your brain thinking ... the perfect way to start the day. Let's get quizzing!

Name the Song

BESTSELLING SINGLES

Put your emoji thinking caps on. It's time to guess the emoji-fication of pop music's bestselling singles. These are a great introduction to emoji puzzles. To help you out, we'll give you a clue: they are all great songs.

1

2

3

4

5

6

7

Name the Song

....

BIG HITS

If you thought that using your emoji-nation to guess the bestselling singles was difficult—you haven't seen anything yet! Can you guess the name of the song from the emoji-fied lyrics?

1

2

3

4

5

6

7

Name the Song

SING-ALONG CLASSICS

There are songs that, even when you just hear the introduction, can make you want to stop what you're doing and sing along to the whole song. Work out the song title from the emoji lyrics ... and then start singing!

1

2

3

4

5

6

7

Name the Song

POP

Known as "ear-worms," these are songs that get stuck in your head. They are so melodic, so catchy, and so irresistible that you'll be singing them all day. Can you guess which emojis make up which song?

1
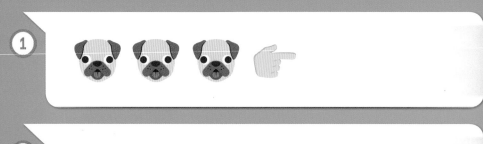

2

3

4

5

6

7

Name the Song

....

CLASSICS

Since the creation of popular chart music in the 1950s, many songs have become undisputed classics; the type of song that even if you've never heard it before, somehow you still know how it goes. These are just those types of songs. Can you work out what they are?

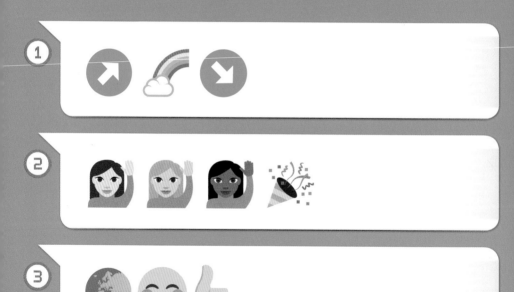

4

5

6

7

Name the Song

FROM THE CHORUS

Catchy melodic choruses are often the greatest part of any song. They can infiltrate our ears and leave us humming them for days. From power ballads to pop operas, punk screams to soulful squeals, can you guess the title of the song from these killer choruses? So, what are you waiting for? Don't bore us; get to the chorus!

1.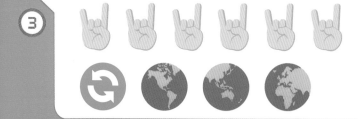

2.

3.

Name the Song

MODERN ANTHEMS

In the 2000s, there was an explosion of new technology that completely changed how we listened to music. The iPod and other MP3 players gave the world freedom to listen to whatever they liked, whenever they wanted, and with the rise of urban, nu-metal and folk troubadours, music had never been so different and so beautiful ...

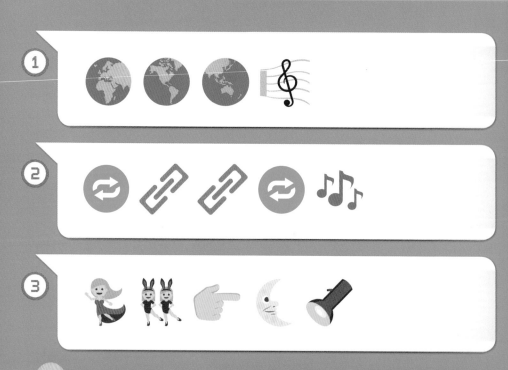

4

5

6

7

Name the Song

1960s CLASSICS

The evolution of modern mainstream popular culture began, as a counter-culture, around the start of the 1960s. It was a time when music really did change the world. Let's celebrate this important moment in time, from 1960 to 1970, by solving these emoji puzzles.

4

5

6

7

Name the Song

1970s CLASSICS

Work out the lyrics and themes of these emoji puzzles to guess the timeless anthems from the most prolific and strangest period of rock and roll—the 1970s. Each one of these tracks features in the Rock and Roll Hall of Fame.

1

2

3

4

5

6

7

Name the Song

1980s–1990s CLASSICS

Since the birth of rock and roll, every decade has delivered more amazing songs than you can shake a stick at. The 50s gave us rock, the 60s gave us soul and the 70s gave us heavy rock. Leave it to the 80s and 90s, then, to give us a combination of all three. Ladies and gentleman, let's go back to the time that no one is ever allowed to forget ... even if they would prefer to!

4

5

6

7

Name the Album Title

ROCK AND ROLL

Within moments of emojis being created, the world descended into complete and total emoji-monium. Emoji-fanatics turned their favorite albums and song titles into emoji form, and emoji-holics on the Internet lapped them up! Remember, don't turn to the answers until you have worked them all out. No cheating allowed!

1

2

3

4

5

6

7

Name the Album Title

....

POP

Pop music and emojis go together like burgers and fries. Many modern pop album titles, and lyrics, are incredibly emoji-friendly. Try these mega-successful album titles on for size ...

①

②

③

1	1	1	1	1	1	1
1	1	1	1	1	1	1
1	1	1	1	1	1	1

6

7

Name the Artist

ROCK AND ROLL

From Elvis Presley to the Beatles, the White Stripes to the Black Keys, rock and roll is the best way to have a good time. Can you work out who these famous artists and bands are?

1

2

3

4

5

6

7

Name the Artist

POP

From Prince to Pink, Madonna to Rihanna, there are some awesome mononyms in the history of pop. But their names aren't the only interesting monikers in music. These musicians and bands have cool names, too. But who are they?

1

2

3

4

5

6

7

Name the Music Video

CLASSICS

When MTV first became an international TV phenomenon, it was amazing to be able to see our favorite pop stars in technicolor on the small screen. Today, these clips have hundreds of millions of hits on YouTube ... but can you identify the videos?

1

2

3

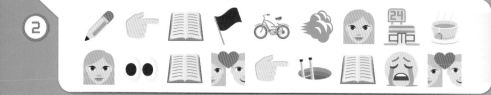

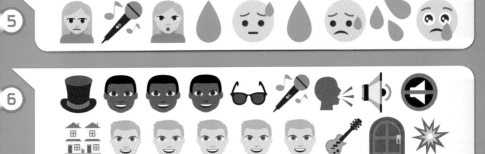

Name the Music Video

MASTERPIECES

With the increase in digital technology, music videos of the past decade have become visual spectaculars that are designed to blow us away. So can you guess these groundbreaking music video "plots"? Each one is as awesome as the last.

2

Movies & TV

The world has gone emoji crazy, we all know that—especially when it comes to emoji-fying classic movies, TV shows and beloved characters. And why not? It's where the stars of the small screen can mingle with the legends of the big screen, too. So, let's sort the *Mad Men* from the *Bad Boys*, the Khaleesis from the *Girls* and start flexing those brain muscles to win some puzzle points. And the award goes to ...

Name the Movie

BLOCKBUSTERS

Every year, several billion-dollar blockbuster movies are unleashed on eager audiences, targeted to thrill and entertain us. Here we have emoji-fied some of the world's greatest blockbuster plots. Can you work out the movie from these emoji stories?

1.

2.

3.

Name the Movie

We're not done yet—here are some more emoji blockbusters to solve!

1

2

3

Movies & TV   49

Name the Movie

DISASTER MOVIES

No cinematic genre takes our collective breath away quite like an epic disaster movie. Like perfect storms and terrifying tornadoes, alien invasions and erupting volcanoes, these emoji puzzles are out to get you. Can you guess the movie and save the day?

1

2

3

Name the Movie

....

SCIENCE FICTION

With ever more sophisticated CGI and improved 3D technology, pretty soon science-fiction movies are going to be taking us to parts of the universe that we have only ever dreamed of. For now, let's keep our minds closer to home and solve these sci-fi emoji puzzles.

1

2

3

4

5

6

7

Name the Movie

COMEDY

There's nothing like a good comedy to tickle our funny bones. There's also nothing better than solving an emoji puzzle ... especially if they remind us of our favorite comedy and give our brain a workout.

1

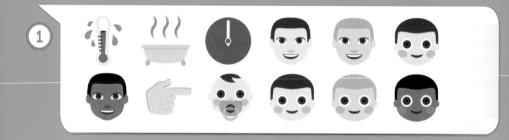

2

3

4

5

6

7

Name the Movie

ACTION AND ADVENTURE

From Jason Bourne to James Bond, Indiana Jones to John McClane, the best action and adventure movies always have us on the edge of our seats, trying to figure out who the bad guy is, and whether the good guy will ultimately win. Be a good guy ... and work out these bad boys!

1

2

3

(4)

(5)

(6)

(7)

Name the Movie

SUPERHEROES

Superhero movies have swung into our lives like Spiderman over recent years and captured our hearts like Iron Man catches bad guys. With new and even stranger superhero movies on the horizon, don't be surprised to see superhero emojis appear very soon, too. Until then, riddle me these, Batman ...

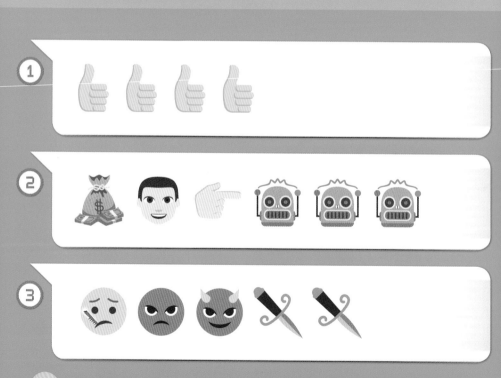

4

5

6

7

Name the Movie

ROM-COMS

There are hundreds of classic rom-coms that have melted our hearts, caused us to cry, and made us wish for that kind of extraordinary romance in our lives. Guess the rom-com emojis below ... and then send someone a heart emoji to let them know you're thinking of them.

1.

2.

3.

4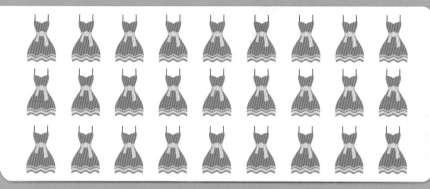

5

6 1 0

7

Name the Movie

....

HORROR AND DRAMA

Tense, scary movies can produce some very intense emotions—and screams—especially when your nightmares appear on the big screen. Work out the emoji puzzles below then treat yourself to a binge-watching session of these classic movies. That's if you can work out what they are ...

1

2

3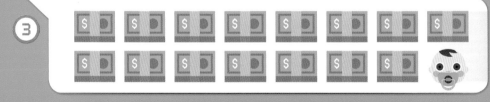

4

5

6

7

Name the Movie

THRILLERS

Car chases, shadowy figures, deception, killer deaths, sneaky twists, and cliffhangers—all these things make for a fantastic thriller that deserves repeat viewings. So, put your emoji thinking cap on and solve these puzzles like a good detective would.

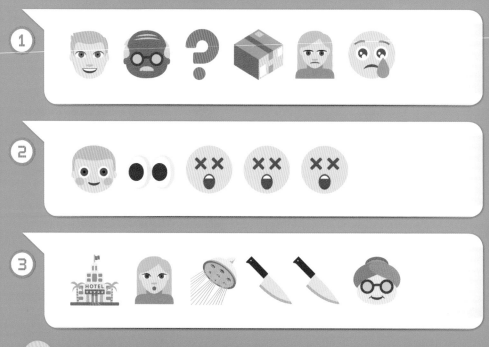

4

5

6

7

Name the Movie

....

ANIMATION

Shrek and Donkey, Woody and Buzz, Simba and Nala. Over the past 20 years, animated movies have given us rich, emotionally intelligent characters that we have come to adore. Guess the animated movie from the emoji puzzles below.

1

2

3

4

5

6

7

Name the Movie

....

MUSICALS AND FAMILY

Musicals and family movies—that's usually enough to make dad groan. But for the rest of us, these two cinematic genres might make us break into song and help us to remember that if life gives you lemons, you make lemonade. All together now ...

1

2

3

Name the Character

....

MAIN CHARACTERS

Characters from the big screen often stick with us long after the movies is over. Whether they're evil or good, loathsome or lovable, there are lots of great characters made famous from the movies ... but can you guess these seven?

1

2

3

4

5

6

7

Name the Character

THE HEROES

Cinema is action-packed with awesome saviors that swoop in to save the damsel or dude in distress, usually just in the nick of time. Can you work out these emoji heroes? Quick, you haven't got long!

1

2

3

4

5

6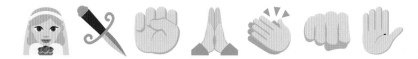

7

Name the Character

THE BAD GUYS

Miscreants, scoundrels, rogues, crooks, criminals, and troublemakers. Whatever you call them, bad guys make evil look good. Of course, they never win—the good guys always swoop in and spoil the fun. But before that happens, can you figure out the villains in these emoji puzzles?

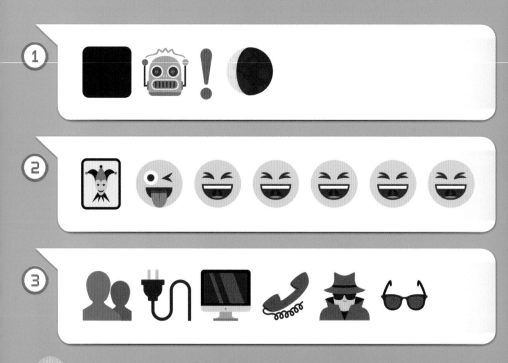

4   ← **END**

5

6

7

Name the Movie Scene

EASY

Every great movie has that standout scene that you look forward to the most. Be it Jack and Rose's first kiss in *Titanic*, Marty McFly's ride on that famous hoverboard in *Back to the Future*, or when Julia Roberts was "just a girl, standing in front of a guy" in *Notting Hill*. Can you work out these famous movie scenes?

1

2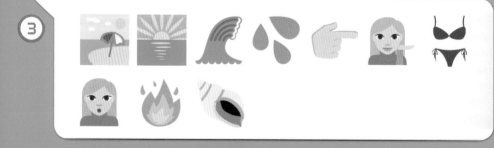

3

4

5

6

7

Name the Movie Quote

EASY

Quoting movies is endlessly enjoyable. With the invention of emojis, you can now do it in style! Try and work out these little gems—some of the greatest lines spoken in the movies.

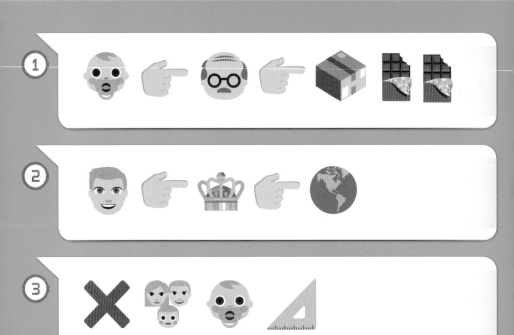

4

5

6

7

Name the Movie Quote

....

MEDIUM

These movie quotes are a little bit harder (unless you're a complete movie buff). The movies are famous, and the quotes are iconic—but the emoji-fication makes them tricky to decipher. Have a go at working out the quotes from these emoji puzzles.

4

5

6

7

Quick-fire Movie Round

EASY

The fuse has been lit. You have ten seconds to solve the emoji puzzles on this page before the lights go out and the world explodes! This message will self-destruct in 10, 9, 8, 7 ... Get thinking!

(1)

(2)

(3)

4

5

6

7

Name the TV Show

Where would we be without TV? It's arguably the greatest invention ever made—along with emojis, of course—and one that has brought us all so much joy. Name the TV shows below, if you can. These ones are easy, right?

1

2

3

4

5

6

7

Name the TV Show

MEDIUM

TV is our friend, and like all good friends, it never lets us down. It's always there when we need it, and it won't tell us off if we binge-watch all day. From zombie apocalypses to police procedurals, love triangles to time-travelling space adventures, TV's got it covered. Now, guess the show ...

1
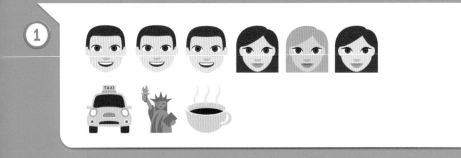

2
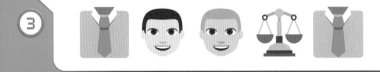

3

(4)

(5)

(6)

(7)

Name the TV Show

. . . .

HARD

Now you've solved those emoji enigmas, try these brain-busting puzzles for size. It's nothing you can't handle—we know you watch enough TV!

1

2

3

4

5

6

7

3

Sports & Culture

When it comes to emoji puzzles, you're either a heavyweight who rolls with the punches, or a lightweight who throws in the towel: there's no room for losers who drop the ball or take a dive in this team. If you can defeat these tricky emoji sports and culture puzzles with a hole-in-one, a slam-dunk or even a sneaky sucker-punch, then the golden prize is yours for the taking. Let's play ball ...

Name the Sports Star

EASY

Many of the world's greatest sports players are revered for their record-breaking achievements and talents—but not all of them. Can you spot the heroes from the villains below?

1

2

3

Name the Sports Star

MEDIUM

There are dozens of awesome sport emojis to choose from. In order to give our brains a workout, let's have a go at some slightly trickier emoji puzzles. Nothing you can't handle, right?

1
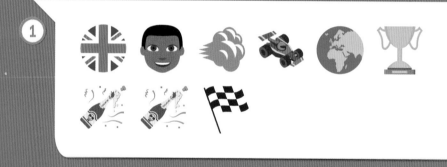

3

4.

5.

6.

7.

Name the Sports Star

HARD

The world's most famous athletes are renowned for their ability to kick the ball in the goal, shoot a hole in one, score an alley-oops, and net awesome shots, sometimes with only seconds to go. Be like them and get these hard emoji puzzles correct in one shot.

1

2

3

4

5

6

7

Name the Sports Star

ADVANCED

As with all sports (and emoji puzzling!), there are some that you may find easier than others. Well, consider the following enigmas to be the heavyweight champions of emoji puzzles, guaranteed to knock you out if you don't stay on your feet. So, who is who?

1

2

3

4

5

6

7

Name the Famous Sporting Event

WORLD

You only have to look at the number of sport emojis there are to know that there are hundreds of awesome sports to play. Can you guess the sporting event from the emoji puzzles below?

1

2

3

4

5

6

7

Name the Famous Sporting Event

SPECIFIC MOMENT

Now for more sporting events, but this time, these emoji puzzles are specific moments in sporting history. So, score a home run, go the distance, and knock these puzzles out of the ballpark ...

4

5

6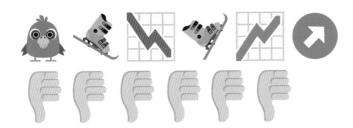

7

Name the Book

EASY

Fairy tales, and other classic children's stories, have endured for centuries, forever passed down through generations. These timeless stories will continue to enthrall us, especially now that they are in emoji! Work them out and pass them on.

1

2

3

Name the Book

MEDIUM

I know what you're thinking. "More books? Boring." Well, you're wrong. Books are fun—especially in emoji form! Hopefully you've read them. If you haven't, you must. Can you guess the titles of these famous, classic books?

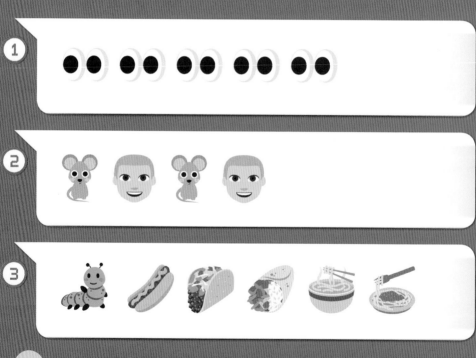

4

5

6

7

Name the Book

HARD

From Roald Dahl to C. S. Lewis, George Orwell to George Eliot, beloved authors have been telling unforgettable tales of love, joy, and adventure for centuries. We look to books for entertainment and enrichment. But forget all that serious stuff for now—can you guess which classic books have been emoji-fied?

4

5

6

7

Name the Book

ADVANCED

These emoji puzzles are advanced and will really test if you're a true bookworm. If you get them all right, give yourself a pat on the back, and move on to the next page. Be a winner!

1

2

3

4

5

6

7

Name the Work of Art

EASY

The world's greatest, and most famous, art masterpieces have survived for many centuries, and are a sight to behold. But, as with all art, beauty is in the eye of the beholder. How many famous emoji art masterpieces can you name?

1

2

3

4

5

6

7

Name the Video Game

EASY

From *Pac-Man* to *The Legend of Zelda*, *Sonic the Hedgehog* to *Call of Duty*, computer games have risen up the ranks to be one of the most popular forms of entertainment in the 21st century. And it's easy to see why, with such a huge range of awesome games to choose from. Are you a gamer? If so, can you name check these famous video games?

1

2

3

4

5

6

7

Name the Historic Event

EASY

Many nations have had important moments in their history that made the world stand up and take notice. These are those events—but in emoji form. Now work them out using your well-honed emoji-knowledge. These are easy.

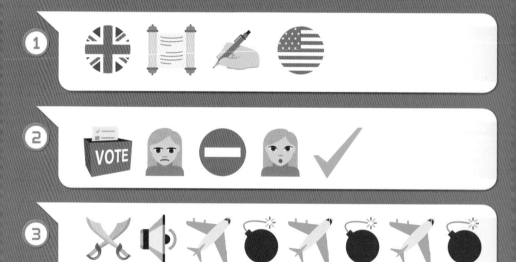

4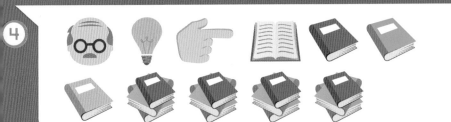

5

6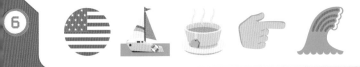

7

Name the Historic Event

MEDIUM

These historic events are a little harder to guess than the previous set. Give yourself a bit longer to work them out.

1

2

3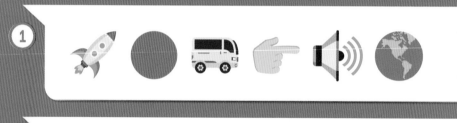

Sports & Culture 119

Name the Historic Event

HARD

These historic events are going to be difficult—they are for the super-smart among you. If you work these out, you've done very well. You better get cracking ... Go!

Name the Scientific Inventor

EASY

In the last century alone, the rapid evolution of science and technology has given us a million-and-one brilliant inventions, inventors and events that have changed the world for the better. Let's celebrate them with the highest form of praise ... emoji-fication! Can you guess the scientific inventor?

1

2

3

4

5

6

7

Name the Scientific Inventor

••

MEDIUM

Newton, Einstein, Tesla, Berners-Lee, Musk. All these brilliantly intelligent and innovative people gave us the opportunity to enjoy our time on earth even more so than ever before. Can you work out these game-changers?

4

5

6

7

4

Trivia & Answers

Congratulations, you have reached the final chapter. You are now an emoji jedi, or an emoji ninja, well versed in the art of emoji puzzling. Once you've caught your breath, it's time to head on down to trivia town and learn everything you wanted to know about emojis but were too afraid to ask. If you're seeking emoji enlightenment, then the answers are on page 140—but shame on you for needing them!

What Does Your Favorite Emoji Say About You?

You may have your own favorite go-to emojis. You know, the ones you send every day, either as your code to tell your friends, or your partner, that you are thinking of them, or as a way to sign off your messages. It could be the Thumbs Up Sign, the Sparkling Heart, or the Grimacing Face. If you have wondered what your favorite emoji says about you, then fear no more, the answers are on their way. Here are some of the world's most popular emojis. Are they yours too?

Data is amazing—especially when it comes to emojis. For instance, did you know that the American state of Colorado uses the book emoji more than any other U.S. state? Or that the German's use the See-No-Evil Monkey emoji more than any other nation? It makes you think—why is this?

Thanks to a 2015 report that analyzed more than one billion emojis sent in the previous year, we are now able to work out and understand where the world's most treasured emojis are sent from, by whom, and perhaps why.

CANADIAN POOP
Once regarded as everybody's favorite emoji, the Pile of Poop is certainly one of the world's most popular forms of emoji expression. However, surprisingly, emoji data suggests that the Pile of Poop emoji is used the most in .... Drum roll ... Canada!

RUSSIAN KISS
Often used instead of "xx" at the end of text messages and online posts, the Kiss Mark is most commonly used in Russia, but is also popular all over the world.

The World's Favorite Emojis

 PARTY POPPER Most popularly used by Italians, the Party Popper is perfect if you are preparing for a fun night out.

 FACE SCREAMING IN FEAR Recently watched a scary movie? Then the Face Screaming in Fear is the perfect emoji. It is popular in the U.S.

 BROKEN HEART The international symbol of breaking up, the Broken Heart emoji is, sadly, one of the most used, especially in Latin Spanish regions.

SMILING FACE WITH HEART-SHAPED EYES The French are known for speaking the language of love, so it's no surprise that France uses four times as many heart emojis than any other country in the world.

SAD FACE Popular in every country, the Sad Face emoji is often deployed at the end of a bad day. It has been sent billions of times to date.

 FACE WITH TEARS OF JOY The world's most used emoji, the Face With Tears of Joy, is the most popular emoji everywhere.

 CLINKING BEER MUGS AND GRINNING FACE Australians use double the amount of alcohol-themed emojis than any other nation. They also love sending the Grinning Face.

 THUMBS UP SIGN We've all sent the Thumbs Up Sign upon hearing good news. It's popular in Malaysia.

FISTED HAND SIGN Popular in Vietnam, the Fisted Hand Sign is also a great way to send your friends a virtual fist bump to let them know they've done well.

 WINKING FACE Famously known for their cheeky behavior, it's no surprise that the Winking Face is most used in the U.K.

Emoji-mania

Emojis are loved all over the world. From becoming everybody's new favorite round at quiz nights, to being deployed (or discussed) to hilarious effect in pretty much every recent TV show or movie, emojis have infiltrated our lives—so much so that we feel attached to them. But what do we really know about them? Let's find out the facts.

THE MEANING OF EMOJI
Emoji, noun: a small digital image or icon used to express an idea or emotion in electronic communication. The origin of the word "emoji" comes from the Japanese translation of "e" meaning "picture" and "moji" meaning "letter or character."

HAPPY DAYS
It is estimated that globally about 45 percent of all emojis sent are happy faces, including the world's most popular emoji—the Face With Tears of Joy, while 14 percent were reported to be sad faces. Thankfully, that means that there are lots of happy emoji users out there! Twelve percent of all emojis sent relate to hearts of various types. Hopefully, only a handful are the Broken Heart.

FATHER OF THE EMOJI
Inspired by manga, Chinese characters, and street signs, a man named Shigetaka Kurita created emojis as a way to make communication easier. They didn't become popular until Apple incorporated the Unicode Standard, the standard of a nonprofit organization that makes sure characters like emojis can be rendered accurately across different computing platforms, in its operating systems.

Kurita wanted to convey emotions and thoughts without the symbols polarizing those who would see them, so he developed emojis to be as clear and straightforward as possible. Eventually, Kurita came up with 176 12×12 pixel images that would eventually be the foundation for emojis everywhere. At the time of print there are 845 different official Apple-based emojis, with more scheduled to be released every year.

WORD OF THE YEAR!
There are more than a million words in the English language, but in 2015 the esteemed fellows at the prestigious Oxford Dictionary Word of the Year program chose the Face With Tears of Joy emoji to be their Word of the Year. While many may have scoffed at the notion, the rest of us cheered in delight that our lovely emoji friends had made an important, and positive impact on society, following hot on the heels of other trendsetting words such as "selfie," "twerk" and "phablet."

EMOJI DICK—THE BOOK
Did you know there is a book written entirely in emojis? It's called *Emoji Dick*. Created and compiled by Fred Benenson, *Emoji Dick* is the world's first emoji-only version of the classic seafaring whale-hunt adventure, *Moby-Dick*, by American novelist Herman Melville.

Emoji-mania

There's more to emojis than meets the eye. Here are even more awesome emoji facts to feast your peepers on.

I HEART EMOJI
In 2014, the Heart emoji destroyed all the competition (i.e. every other word) and became the most frequently used word in the English language, across all published print and digital media.

EMOJINARY
Emoticons, and very basic emojis, have been popular worldwide since the year 1999, but they only became superstars that we could no longer live without in 2012, thanks in part to the emoji keyboard on Apple's iPhone 4. The word "emoji" was promptly added to the Oxford Dictionary in 2013. Since then, emojis have competed with selfies to be the world's biggest and most enduring digital trend!

WORLD EMOJI DAY
July 17 has been deemed World Emoji Day. Every year this date will be revered for its celebration of all things emoji. On this day, sending lots of emojis to your friends and family is not only justified—but also compulsory! But why July 17, we hear you ask. Well, take a look at the calendar emoji in your emoji keyboard. It always says July 17. Why? It's in honor of the launch of Apple's digital calendar iCal, which was released on, you guessed it, July 17, 2002.

EMOJI SECURITY

Forget having to remember pin codes as complicated as "1, 2, 3, 4" or, "Password1." In the future you may soon be able to create passwords that you'll really remember—for example "Dragon Face, Cactus, Crying Face." That's if the British software company Intelligent Environments gets its way, at least. The company has petitioned for emoji passwords to be introduced to personal banking systems. Sounds ridiculous? Don't laugh: it's actually incredibly sensible. With 44 official emojis to choose from, the password combination options run into the trillions, thus increasing security for all. What would your emoji password be?

EMOJI MADNESS

As of early 2016 threatening someone (which you should never do, obviously) by using certain emojis could land you into serious trouble. For the first time ever, courts in Europe and the U.S. are admitting emojis such as the Pistol, the Bomb, and the Skull as evidence of threatening behavior. Be careful what you send!

VISIOSUBRIDEOPHOBIA

Try saying this word—visiosubrideophobia—five times, fast! Yes, you've probably guessed it, but visiosubrideophobia is the fear of smiling faces, commonly associated with a dislike of emojis and emoticons. For those suffering from this phobia, receiving an emoji message can be unnerving.

Emoji-mania

The emoji craze has only just started and in case you're not completely stuffed on emoji facts right now, here is a handful more to keep you well and truly emoji-educated. Did you know ...

EMOJI TRACKER
If you want to keep an eye on a particular usage of a certain emoji—at any time—or observe how many people around the world are Tweeting a certain emoji then you can do just that. Head over to emojitracker.com and witness "an experiment in real-time visualization" (their words) of all the emojis being used on Twitter in real-time. As you can imagine, emojis are used more frequently in the evening and Angry Face is deployed heavily whenever there is a sports match on. Emoji Tracker constantly updates with Twitter, so you can see the number count rise and slow beside each emoji.

THE EMOJI MOVIE
Following hot on the heels of *Warcraft* and *The Angry Birds Movie* released in 2016, Sony Pictures Animation has officially announced that in 2017, *The Emoji Movie* will be released. The first major emoji movie is certainly expected to raise some eyebrows and all eyes are focused on what the plot will be and, most importantly, who will star or voice the emojis. It's a movie we'd all love to go and see!

EMOJI-MENTARY
If buying a book about emojis is your first step to emoji nirvana, then you should also check out the really cool documentary *Emoji Among Us* on Vimeo. This short movie highlights how important emojis are in our society today, how we need to communicate with each other now, and how they can help spread positive change around the world.

EMOJI DELIVERY
With the emoji craze in full swing, in 2016 the popular pizza delivery brand Dominos was one the first standout examples of a company turning to emojis to help sell their product. Trialed in early 2016, the new online and smartphone-operated ordering system from Domino's allowed hungry users to text a pizza emoji to a Domino's number and place a pre-saved delivery order. How amazing is that? It's likely that pretty soon other major companies will follow suit and before you know it, everyone will be emoji-ordering their food and consumer products with the touch of an emoji.

IMOJI
Have you heard of Imoji? No? Well, your world is about to get a whole lot cooler! Imoji, one of the latest emoji apps, lets you turn your photos into sticker emojis that you can insert into your messages and send to whoever you like. It's simple! Download the app, choose a photo, use your finger to trace around the photo you want to send and, *voila*! It is transformed into a sticker emoji that you can send to friends.

Quiz Night Questions

QUICK-FIRE ROUND: SINGLE-PLAYER

As you have successfully made it this far, like at any good quiz night, it's time to take the quick-fire round. There are no clues. You just have to figure out what on earth is going on through the emojis. On your marks, get set, go!

(1)

(2)

(3)

4

5

6

7

Quiz Night Questions

QUICK-FIRE ROUND: MULTIPLAYER

This round is slightly different. Instead of trying to solve these puzzles yourself, message each one of the seven puzzles to seven separate friends at the same time. Apps, TV shows, movie plots, books—the answers could be anything. The first one to reply with the correct answers wins ... nothing—except your respect!

1

2

3

4

5

6

7

Answers

Chapter One: Music
• • • • • • • • • • • • • • • • • •

12–13 Name the Song
BESTSELLING SINGLES
1. "Set Fire to the Rain"
2. "Uptown Funk"
3. "Thinking Out Loud"
4. "American Pie"
5. "Cry Me a River"
6. "Stairway to Heaven"
7. "Clocks"

14–15 Name the Song
BIG HITS
1. "Firework"
2. "Never Gonna Give You Up"
3. "This Love"
4. "Wrecking Ball"
5. "Drunk in Love"
6. "Happy"
7. "Bad Blood"

16–17 Name the Song
SING-ALONG CLASSICS
1. "U Can't Touch This"
2. "Hello"
3. "When Doves Cry"
4. "Wake Me up Before You Go-Go"
5. "Ticket to Ride"
6. "I Still Haven't Found What I'm Looking For"
7. "Hotline Bling"

18–19 Name the Song
POP
1. "Who Let the Dogs Out?"
2. "Chasing Cars"
3. "Single Ladies (Put a Ring on It)"
4. "Poker Face"

5. "Take Me to Church"
6. "I Kissed a Girl"
7. "Can't Get You Out of My Head"

20–21 Name the Song
CLASSICS
1. "Somewhere Over the Rainbow"
2. "Girls Just Want to Have Fun"
3. "What a Wonderful World"
4. "Seven Nation Army"
5. "My Heart Will Go On"
6. "...Baby One More Time"
7. "It's Raining Men"

22–23 Name the Song
FROM THE CHORUS
1. "China in Your Hand"
2. "Everybody (Backstreet's Back)"
3. "Rockin' All Over the World"
4. "Rehab"
5. "Do they Know it's Christmas?"
6. "(I Just) Died in Your Arms Tonight"
7. "Get Lucky"

24–25 Name the Song
MODERN ANTHEMS
1. "Earth Song"
2. "Unchained Melody"
3. "Dancing in the Moonlight"
4. "Don't Look Back in Anger"
5. "Love Will Tear Us Apart"
6. "2 Become 1"
7. "Smells Like Teen Spirit"

26–27 Name the Song
1960s CLASSICS
1. "Blowin' in the Wind"
2. "House of the Rising Sun"
3. "I Heard it Through the Grapevine"

4. "You've Lost That Lovin' Feeling"
5. "The Lion Sleeps Tonight"
6. "Jumpin' Jack Flash"
7. "Pretty Woman"

28–29 Name the Song
1970s CLASSICS
1. "Raindrops Keep Fallin' On My Head"
2. "The Long and Winding Road"
3. "Ain't No Mountain High Enough"
4. "The Tears of A Clown"
5. "Band on the Run"
6. "Dancing Queen"
7. "How Deep is Your Love?"

30–31 Name the Song
1980–1990s CLASSICS
1. "Total Eclipse of the Heart"
2. "Everybody Wants to Rule the World"
3. "The Power Of Love"
4. "We Built This City"
5. "Walk Like an Egyptian"
6. "Ice Ice Baby"
7. "End of the Road"

32–33 Name the Album Title
ROCK AND ROLL
1. *(What's the Story) Morning Glory?*
2. *Highway to Hell*
3. *Pet Sounds*
4. *The Blueprint*
5. *Born to Run*
6. *Back to Black*
7. *Songs in the Key of Life*

34–35 Name the Album Title
POP
1. *Like a Prayer*
2. *Dangerously in Love*

3. *21*
4. *Bat Out of Hell*
5. *The Man Who Sold the World*
6. *Oops! I Did it Again*
7. *Love. Angel. Music. Baby.*

36−37 Name the Artist
ROCK AND ROLL
1. The Doors
2. Arctic Monkeys
3. Snoop Dogg
4. Imagine Dragons
5. OK Go
6. Rage Against the Machine
7. Earth, Wind & Fire

38−39 Name the Artist
POP
1. One Direction
2. Michael Jackson
3. 5 Seconds of Summer
4. The Police
5. The Beach Boys
6. Red Hot Chili Peppers
7. Eminem

40−41 Name the Music Video
CLASSICS
1. "Thriller"
2. "Take on Me"
3. "Cryin'"
4. "Sabotage"
5. "Nothing Compares 2 U"
6. "Walk this Way"
7. "Always"

42−43 Name the Music Video
MASTERPIECES
1. "Da Funk"
2. "Yellow"
3. "Learn to Fly"
4. "Bittersweet Symphony"

5. "What's My Age Again?"
6. "Wicked Game"
7. "Weapon of Choice"

Chapter Two: Movies & TV
•••••••••••••••••••••••••••••

46−47 Name the Movie
BLOCKBUSTERS
1. *Back to the Future*
2. *Titanic*
3. *Speed*
4. *Jurassic Park*
5. *Transformers*
6. *Gone With the Wind*
7. *Apollo 13*

48−49 Name the Movie
BLOCKBUSTERS
1. *The Bourne Identity*
2. *Alice in Wonderland*
3. *Fight Club*
4. *Up*
5. *The Sound of Music*
6. *The Karate Kid*

50−51 Name the Movie
DISASTER MOVIES
1. *The Day After Tomorrow*
2. *Twister*
3. *War of the Worlds*
4. *Zombieland*
5. *Arachnophobia*
6. *Deep Impact*
7. *Outbreak*

52−53 Name the Movie
SCIENCE FICTION
1. *Interstellar*
2. *Twelve Monkeys*
3. *Star Wars*
4. *E.T. the Extra-Terrestrial*
5. *The Matrix*

6. *Cowboys & Aliens*
7. *Inception*

54−55 Name the Movie
COMEDY
1. *Hot Tub Time Machine*
2. *Home Alone*
3. *Men in Black*
4. *Big*
5. *Ghostbusters*
6. *Trading Places*
7. *Dude, Where's My Car?*

56−57 Name the Movie
ACTION AND ADVENTURE
1. *Taken*
2. *The Lord of the Rings*
3. *Casino Royale*
4. *Everest*
5. *Furious 7*
6. *Jurassic World*
7. *300*

58−59 Name the Movie
SUPERHEROES
1. *Fantastic Four*
2. *Iron Man 3*
3. *Deadpool*
4. *Captain America*
5. *Superman*
6. *Thor*
7. *Spiderman*

60−61 Name the Movie
ROM-COMS
1. *Knocked Up*
2. *Four Weddings and a Funeral*
3. *Groundhog Day*
4. *Date Night*
5. *27 Dresses*
6. *10 Things I Hate About You*
7. *Six Days, Seven Nights*

62–63 Name the Movie
HORROR AND DRAMA
1. *Bridge of Spies*
2. *The Exorcist*
3. *Million Dollar Baby*
4. *Castaway*
5. *Raging Bull*
6. *The Wizard of Oz*
7. *The Silence of the Lambs*

64–65 Name the Movie
THRILLERS
1. *Seven*
2. *The Sixth Sense*
3. *Psycho*
4. *No Country for Old Men*
5. *Fatal Attraction*
6. *The Shining*
7. *Kiss Kiss Bang Bang*

66–67 Name the Movie
ANIMATION
1. *Finding Nemo*
2. *Monsters, Inc.*
3. *How to Train Your Dragon*
4. *Chicken Run*
5. *Kung Fu Panda*
6. *Cloudy with a Chance of Meatballs*
7. *Ratatouille*

68–69 Name the Movie
MUSICALS AND FAMILY
1. *Mary Poppins*
2. *Babe: Pig in the City*
3. *Frozen*
4. *Pinocchio*
5. *The Jungle Book*
6. *Antz*
7. *The Princess and the Frog*

70–71 Name the Character
MAIN CHARACTERS
1. James Bond
2. Ferris Bueller
3. Terminator
4. Forrest Gump
5. Wolverine
6. Ace Ventura
7. Buzz Lightyear

72–73 Name the Character
THE HEROES
1. Ellen Ripley
2. Han Solo
3. The Blues Brothers
4. Blade
5. Katniss Everdeen
6. The Bride
7. Doc Brown

74–75 Name the Character
THE BAD GUYS
1. Darth Vader
2. The Joker
3. Agent Smith
4. Ernst Blofeld
5. Ivan Drago
6. Angel Eyes
7. Sauron

76–77 Name the Movie Scene
EASY
1. Marilyn Monroe's dress blowing in the gust of wind from the subway grate in *The Seven Year Itch*.
2. The crop-dusting plane scene in *North by Northwest*.
3. Ursula Andress emerging from the water in *Dr. No*.
4. E.T. and Elliott's bicycle ride in *E.T. the Extra-Terrestrial*.
5. Samara crawling out of the TV in *The Ring*.
6. The parapsychologists encountering a ghost in the library in *Ghostbusters*.
7. Gandalf shouting, "You shall not pass" to Balrog in *The Lord of the Rings: The Fellowship of the Ring*.

78–79 Name the Movie Quote
EASY
1. "Life is like a box of chocolates."
2. "I'm the king of the world!"
3. "Nobody puts Baby in a corner."
4. "If you build it, he will come."
5. "I'll have what she's having."
6. "The greatest trick the devil ever pulled was convincing the world he didn't exist."
7. "I'll be back."

80–81 Name the Movie Quote
MEDIUM
1. "There's no crying in baseball."
2. "Here's looking at you, kid."
3. "You talkin' to me?"
4. "There's no place like home."
5. "I love the smell of napalm in the morning."
6. "Show me the money!"
7. "You're gonna need a bigger boat."

82–83 Quick-fire Movie Round
EASY
1. *Blade Runner*
2. *Nightmare on Elm Street*
3. *Pirates of the Caribbean*
4. *Goldfinger*
5. *The Hangover*
6. *American Beauty*
7. *The Avengers*

84–85 Name the TV Show
EASY
1. *Girls*
2. *House of Cards*
3. *The Office*
4. *The X-Files*
5. *Agents of S.H.I.E.L.D.*
6. *Orange is the New Black*
7. *Mad Men*

86–87 Name the TV Show
MEDIUM
1. *Friends*
2. *The Walking Dead*
3. *Suits*
4. *Doctor Who*
5. *Saved by the Bell*
6. *Star Trek*
7. *Six Feet Under*

88–89 Name the TV Show
HARD
1. *Lost*
2. *Monty Python's Flying Circus*
3. *The Fresh Prince of Bel-Air*
4. *Game of Thrones*
5. *Happy Days*
6. *Brooklyn Nine-Nine*
7. *The Big Bang Theory*

Chapter Three: Sports & Culture
• • • • • • • • • • • • • • • •

92–93 Name the Sports Stars
EASY
1. Muhammad Ali
2. Tiger Woods
3. Usain Bolt
4. Lance Armstrong
5. Sir Steve Redgrave
6. David Beckham
7. Diego Maradona

94–95 Name the Sports Star
MEDIUM
1. Lewis Hamilton
2. Andy Murray
3. Lionel Messi
4. Michael Jordan
5. Michael Phelps
6. Wayne Gretzky
7. Babe Ruth

96–97 Name the Sports Star
HARD
1. Sir Bradley Wiggins
2. Artem Ivanov
3. Seve Ballesteros
4. Jonny Wilkinson
5. Maria Sharapova
6. Tom Brady
7. Lin Dan

98–99 Name the Sports Star
ADVANCED
1. Venus Williams
2. Mo Farah
3. Pelé
4. Tom Daley
5. Ronda Rousey
6. Thierry Henry
7. Shane Warne

100–101 Name the Famous Sporting Event
WORLD
1. Kentucky Derby
2. Summer Olympics
3. Six Nations Rugby Union
4. Super Bowl
5. Tour de France
6. FIFA World Cup
7. Masters Golf Tournament

102–103 Name the Famous Sporting Event
SPECIFIC MOMENT
1. World Cup Final 1966: England v West Germany.
2. 1980 Winter Olympics "Miracle on Ice": USA v Soviet Union.
3. 1984 Winter Olympics: Torvill and Dean became highest scoring figure skaters.
4. Evander Holyfield vs. Mike Tyson II: "The Bite Fight."
5. First sub-4-minute mile: Roger Bannister.
6. 2013 Wimbledon Men's Final: Djokovic v Murray.
7. 1988 Winter Olympics: "Eddie the Eagle" gets lowest scores.

104–105 Name the Book
EASY
1. *Cinderella*
2. *Snow White Seven Dwarfs*
3. *Goldilocks and Three Bears*
4. *The Boy Who Cried Wolf*
5. *Hansel and Gretel*
6. *Little Red Riding Hood*
7. *The Three Little Pigs*

106–107 Name the Book
MEDIUM
1. *1984*
2. *Of Mice and Men*
3. *The Very Hungry Caterpillar*
4. *War and Peace*
5. *The Lion, the Witch and the Wardrobe*
6. *The Tiger Who Came for Tea*
7. *Charlie and the Chocolate Factory*

108–109 Name the Book
HARD
1. *Treasure Island*
2. *James and the Giant Peach*
3. *The Hobbit*
4. *Moby-Dick*
5. *Winnie-the-Pooh*
6. *A Clockwork Orange*
7. *The Grapes of Wrath*

110–111 Name the Book
ADVANCED
1. *Catch-22*
2. *And Then There Were None*
3. *The Da Vinci Code*
4. *Guess How Much I Love You*
5. *Black Beauty*
6. *The Hitchhiker's Guide to the Galaxy*
7. *Heart of Darkness*

112–113 Name the Famous Work of Art
EASY
1. *Mona Lisa*
2. *The Persistence of Memory*
3. *The Starry Night*
4. *The Creation of Adam*
5. *The Scream*
6. *The Last Supper*
7. *Girl With a Balloon*

114–115 Name the Video Game
EASY
1. *Minecraft*
2. *Grand Theft Auto*
3. *Tetris*
4. *Super Mario Kart*
5. *Donkey Kong*
6. *Space Invaders*
7. *Prince of Persia: The Sands of Time*

116–117 Name the Historic Event
EASY
1. The Declaration of Independence
2. Women's right to vote
3. The Blitz
4. Invention of printing press
5. Splitting the atom
6. The Boston Tea Party
7. Man landing on the Moon

118–119 Name the Historic Event
MEDIUM
1. Mars Rover
2. Prohibition in the United States
3. "I Have A Dream," speech by Martin Luther King Jr.
4. The Beatles arrive in the United States
5. Darwin's Theory of Evolution
6. Invention of the Internet

120–121 Name the Historic Event
HARD
1. Assassination of John F. Kennedy
2. Roswell UFO crash at Area 51
3. Christopher Columbus discovers America
4. Death of the dinosaurs
5. Invention of the light bulb
6. Isaac Newton's Universal Law of Gravitation
7. English fleet defeats Spanish Armada

122–123 Name the Scientific Inventor
EASY
1. Albert Einstein
2. Archimedes
3. Galileo Galilei
4. Benjamin Franklin
5. Alexander Graham Bell
6. Nicolaus Copernicus
7. Henry Ford

124–125 Name the Scientific Inventor
MEDIUM
1. Cai Lun
2. Steve Jobs
3. Marie Curie
4. Samuel Morse
5. James Watt
6. William Cullen
7. Humphry Davy

Chapter Four: Trivia
● ● ● ● ● ● ● ● ● ● ● ● ● ● ● ● ● ● ●

136–137 Quiz Night Questions
QUICK-FIRE ROUND: SINGLE-PLAYER
1. *The Revenant*
2. Dolly the Sheep
3. Simon Cowell
4. *The Simpsons*
5. *Breaking Bad*
6. Amelia Earhart
7. *Frankenstein*

138–139 Quiz Night Questions
QUICK-FIRE ROUND: MULTIPLAYER
1. *American Horror Story*
2. *On the Road*
3. *Raiders of the Lost Ark*
4. *Happy Gilmore*
5. *Angry Birds*
6. *Phantom of the Opera*
7. St. Patrick's Day

Emoji artwork supplied by Emoji One (http://emojione.com)